Therefore, if anyone is in Christ,
the new creation has come...

Turning Over a New Leaf

Out of the Closet and into the Light

My Story

by

TERI LEEF

Therefore, if anyone is in Christ,
the new creation has come...

WestBow
PRESS
A DIVISION OF THOMAS NELSON

WestBow Press books may be ordered through booksellers or by contacting:

WestBow Press
A Division of Thomas Nelson
1663 Liberty Drive
Bloomington, IN 47403
www.westbowpress.com
1-(866) 928-1240

Art by Sandra Sell from New Hampshire www.Sandrasell.com
http://sandrasell.com/about-the-artist

ISBN: 978-1-4497-9685-3 (sc)
ISBN: 978-1-4497-9686-0 (hc)
ISBN: 978-1-4497-9684-6 (e)

Library of Congress Control Number: 2013909725

Printed in the United States of America.

WestBow Press rev. date: 06/11/2013

Acknowledgments

Thanks so much, Nelda Lockamy, for urging me to write my story so others can be encouraged and benefit from it.

Pastor Homer Murdock and Barbara: I thank God for your loving encouragement and your suggestion of a "God-inspired" title.

For Sandra Sell, my artist friend: Your sketches infused "life" into the book...what a blessing to reunite our friendship after more than twenty years apart!

To Joanne Fletcher, my friend and sister in Christ, I am grateful for your kind assistance in my other businesses in order to free up my time for the project.

Thanks to my new friend and sister in Christ, Joy Lewis, who helped smooth out some rough edges in the edits while currently working on your own book, *The Whisperings of Gilead*.

To friends, Barry & Donna Nealy, thank you for inspiring me in my walk with Christ and for Donna's time in editing and completing the project.

Contents

Part 1

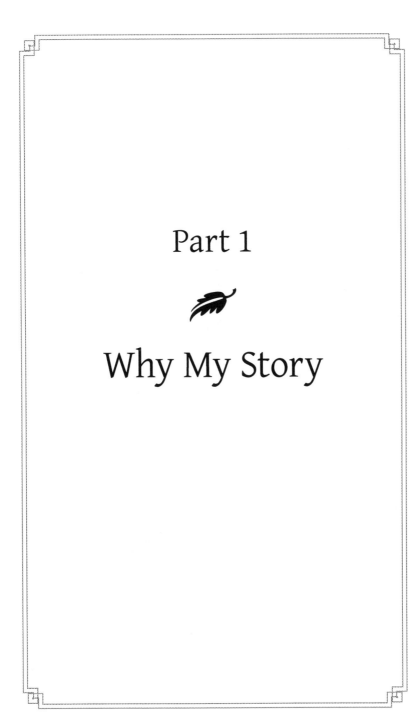

Why My Story

Introduction

The following is **My Testimony** of how God has delivered me and healed me. It is my life story. He delivered me out of a life of darkness and took me out of Satan's hands, and He has been with me throughout my life, although most of the time I never knew He was there.

If it didn't have a beautiful ending, my story would be too painful to tell. I was sexually abused, emotionally abused by family members (including my father, certain older brothers, uncles, and a brother-in-law). When men raped and abused me throughout my formative years it served to warp my sexuality and turned my affections away from men. When my mother neglected to rescue me and comfort me, it caused me great pain, and as a result I sought the love and affection of nurturing females. Over 40 years ago, becoming gay and different stood out like a sore thumb. I became the "black sheep" of my family and was ridiculed at school. To be an "outcast" was very demoralizing, depressing, and painful, and the emotional pain ran deep. While alcohol and drugs could only numb the pain, I did my best to keep it deadened most of the time and the end result was that I became a habitual drunkard and eventually a druggie. Unfortunately, suicide often seemed like my best escape. Even though I tried several times, I never managed to complete it.....what chance did a kid like me have for a happy ending? Without God my chances were slim to none, but when God pursues you, He doesn't give up easily. All things are possible through His grace and love.

I was confused about whether or not I was "born gay" because I had feelings of attraction towards the same sex. I was called names, told that I was going through a phase, and even that I should have been born a man.

I have since learned that sexual orientation is not an "identity" which can be traced to one's genetic makeup. Instead, it is an inclination, desire, or feeling that can usually be traced to a combination of biology and early childhood experiences. Some blame biology for the tendencies of some males who feel the need to be feminine and that of some women who feel the need to be masculine......I found this to be more like role-playing. These tendencies are sometimes minor or hidden, but perceived to be very real.

As in my case, early childhood experiences (such as physical and/or sexual abuse) turned me away from the opposite sex. Other experiences such as the failure of a mother to love, protect, and nurture her daughter, or of a father to foster a loving relationship with his son may turn a person towards the same sex. It is critical to recognize that these experiences are not caused by God. Satan's influence on our lives brings about destructive and sinful consequences.

In fact, people are not "born gay":
- Temptation is not a sin, but what one does in terms of lust and sexual behavior can lead to sin.
- God is not to be blamed for your choices.

The Bible teaches that homosexuality is wrong. Contrary to the popular belief held by many Christians today, homosexuality is not the most heinous of sins and is not the unpardonable sin. **Christ died for all sin!** His blood covers all sin when one seeks His forgiveness. I have come to understand that no matter how "loving" a homosexual relationship is, it is sinful in the eyes of God. Redefinition by government cannot make marriage between same sexes right. God's law defines marriage, not local customs, or laws.

There Is Hope

Because of where I have been, I have a great desire to share my story and show others that there is hope for anyone who is gay or is recovering from a gay lifestyle and may feel hopeless. This hope is there for **anyone** who is hopeless – those addicted to drugs, alcohol, gambling, and sex. *"This is what the Sovereign LORD, the Holy One of Israel, says: In repentance and rest is your salvation, in quietness and trust is your strength, but you would have none of it." Isaiah 30:15.*

My message is intended to say – don't give up, I have been where you are many times before *"For they did not believe in God or trust in his deliverance. In spite of all this, they kept on sinning; in spite of his wonders, they did not believe. So he ended their days in futility and their years in terror." Psalm 78:22, 32-33.*

I want you to know that the same Lord, who helped me out of the pit I was in, is available to help anyone. **He met me where I was**. He has a purpose for my life. *"The Lord God is with you, the Mighty Warrior who saves." Zephaniah 3:17.*

Part 2

Family Turmoil

My Family Background

I was born in the early 60's. I was next to the youngest child… one of eight. I always felt it was my job to protect my baby sister, and I did the best that I could.

I am the only one in my family that is not married, and as an incest survivor, I do not have any children that lived. To my knowledge, only three members of my family have accepted Jesus Christ as Lord and Savior of their lives, and with eight siblings, we're talking about a large extended family! My nephew, Israel, is also a born-again Christian, and both Israel and I were labeled the "black sheep" of our families. My cousin, Jacob, has also given his life to Christ.

The Beginnings of My Abuse

My first encounter with sexual abuse was at the age of six by a brother-in-law who forced me to perform oral sex on him. I have flashbacks of having a beer between my legs – drinking as we were driving out of town. It was after dark, and we were going to get pine trees to plant in our yard. At the farm, he made me go with him into the woods where the dirty deed was done. Later, when I was at least twenty years old, I cut down the specific tree he and I planted in my yard from that farm. What a release I experienced when the chainsaw ripped into that tree, but the memory never ends.

My first encounter with parental neglect was when my baby sister and I were allowed to go with some strangers who had just moved into the neighborhood. We got into trouble with our grade-school principal because of leaving school with these strangers who ended up physically and sexually abusing us.

My parent's priorities were made clear when they served us food from dented cans that tasted of metal. They chose to spend their money on alcohol while much better food was served to those with whom they chose to party. Gambling was a much greater concern than their children. Worst of all, they failed to protect me from the sexual and physical abuse of my brothers.

My parents didn't care if strangers tucked us in at night, or even if they fondled us. I longed for my mother to come to my room at night and ease the covers around me…to assure me that she loved me. They were so busy having sex – NOT behind the closed bedroom door… normal parental sex – but with someone who happened to be there that night. They spent their time getting drunk and bickering and didn't care if we were safe or not. It made no difference that the next day was a school day, and as a result I often fell asleep in school. Again, I was labeled as having a behavior issue – an attitude of not caring about my school work. Young and defenseless, my baby sis and I reaped the darkness of my parents' behavior.

I remember calling my dad at work to see when he was coming home for he would stay there playing cards day after day. This continued year after year, and you knew when my dad lost playing cards – boy did you know! His eyes were brown, but when he came home after losing, they were blacker than black…and then he would beat me, my baby sis, and my mom.

Food For Thought

I have painful memories from my early childhood – but I am not alone. At times I have found myself thinking, "This is all a nightmare!"

On The Table and Under the Light

Sandra F Hill

*My baby sister was behind me in the closet as I
was hiding her as best I could. I could hear them
coming... I wanted someone to help us!*

The sexual abuse of my baby sister and me began in earnest
when I was only six years old. Mom would pull us out of
the closet and put us on the top step of the cellar stairs. At first,

my baby sister asked me why mom put us there. I assured her, "Not to worry, daddy is down there and he won't let anything happen to us." But I didn't know what those filthy, toothless old men with cigar smells and alcohol breath were about to do to us! These were the people he brought home from the nightclubs. They brought us downstairs and laid us upon two separate tables, stripped us down and molested us. There were lights hanging over us so they could see what they were doing. We had been sold (prostituted) by my dad for the fondling/touching/sexual desires of dirty old men. Nothing can take away that feeling! A bubble bath can only remove the outward dirt – what's deep inside remains and causes a lasting impression! To this day, I find myself compulsively cleaning everything – the inside pain was not changed by water then or even by the passing of time. It's bad enough to be molested yourself, but it hurts much worse to see it happen to your baby sister.

Food For Thought

At the time I was being molested, I didn't know God – and if I had, I'm not sure that anyone could have convinced me that He was there. I later learned that God was always listening and watching, and He always had His hand on me.

Missing Sister Found in Courtroom

At the age of five or six years old I remember my baby sister was missing. When I asked my parents where she was, they did not answer me, and she didn't come home......for months!

They took me to a courtroom downtown where I remember seeing the judge on his bench and two men dressed in suits standing in the courtroom with us. I was with both of my parents and when I happened to look over my right shoulder there was my baby sister. She looked at me and smiled from ear to ear. We did all we could not to run to one another! We just smiled and winked at each other. The next thing I heard was the judge saying, "Mr. and Mrs. Leef, you gave birth to eight children, and you're going back home with that eighth child." I saw what seemed like a hundred pieces of paper flying in the air. The people attempting to adopt my baby sister had lost! My parents were actually trying to give my baby sister up for adoption. Their excuse was that they didn't like her behavior, when, in actuality, they were the ones with the behavior problem. When my baby sister met me, we hugged and I did not ever want to let her go again! I never wanted to miss her again like I did during those months!

Food For Thought

I loved my sister and felt responsible for her. God loved her more. His plans for her were not what I would have chosen. In later years she went to church every day. She sought refuge there. She despised drinking and drugs and was able to have a good time without them. The time came when she was gone from my life again; she died at a very early age. God saw fit to give her a perfect home in Heaven... this time He took her to His home.

Taxi from Hell Arrives at Our House

The abuse I experienced was not only physical and sexual. One of my early memories of emotional abuse was a traumatic experience where my dad beat my mom like there was no tomorrow. A woman who lived in our neighborhood arrived at our house one night in a taxi and knocked on the door. She had her belongings with her and was ready to move in with us. My mom threw a fit! Dad was bringing in a new sexual playmate. My mom was going through menopause, and she no longer offered him the satisfaction he desired. When she protested, he blackened my mom's eyes and bloodied her mouth and beat her like a punching bag. I was on his back trying to get him off of her, but there was nothing I could do to save my mom. He threw me into a window and it's a miracle that I didn't break through to the shallow pool two-stories below. He beat my mom – He beat her to a bloody pulp.

At that point in my life I hated her for locking me and my baby sis in the cellar with my dad so he could molest us, but my mother was a pitiful sight that night – I pitied her. She hadn't protected me from my dad or offered to comfort me in any way, but my dad's brutality brought me to the point that I actually felt sorry for her.

Food For Thought

Emotional scars are just as real as physical ones.

Uncle

My mom's brother came to live with us when I was about ten. He did odd jobs around the house and lived in a homemade wooden camper that one of my brothers built beside our house. Uncle used to take me into his camper and force me to bring sexual satisfaction to him with my hands. How? He would threaten that he would find full satisfaction by forcing me, if I didn't do what he asked. How warped is it to tell a ten year old girl that, if she doesn't please him, she will be raped?

Several times, he took me and my baby sis to porno flicks at the drive-in. Dad and Mom knew where he was taking us and allowed it. My sister was so young that it took no time for her to go to sleep in the back seat. I would be sitting there biting my nails knowing what was coming. He would come on to me sexually, but I would pretend to be sick. I really didn't have to do much pretending. He would grumble at me, complaining that he had wasted his money and got nothing in return. But he did leave me alone. What a miracle! I couldn't tell my parents, because they wouldn't take my word over my Uncle's. They wouldn't even take my baby sister's word if she saw something.

Food For Thought

There was no one that I could turn to for protection. I couldn't even trust my own family, but, God was there when I didn't even realize it. He was allowing my testimony to unfold. It was impossible to see then, but I would not trade it for anything now. The ugliness of the hard times has made the beauty of the good times even better. The good times – those have come through Christ.

Party House

Our house was known for all the free alcohol you could drink and all the free food you could eat. They may not have fed us well, but they put out the good stuff for their party pals.

Dad kept ten cases of beer on hand, and plenty of hard liquor was imbibed every weekend. Mixed drinks were prepared ahead of time and often kept in the refrigerator. I had many older siblings as well as nephews and nieces not much younger than myself. Once, someone grabbed orange juice and vodka and put it in one of my nephew's bottles. He could have died from alcohol poisoning!

Each and every Sunday we had about 20 to 30 people come over. We ate in shifts. With time on their hands, there were fist fights, yelling, throwing things, and screaming over each other. No one knew how to have a normal conversation or how to sit and relax and talk, because they were too belligerent most of the time. In the end, my dad would always say, "Forgive and forget… let bygones be bygones…love your brother…" What hypocrisy!

By the age of ten, I would start drinking at 7 AM on a Sunday and be drunk by noon. I was drowning myself with beer and liquor. My family would poke fun at me for being the "black sheep" of the family. All the while, they were sitting there drinking, partying, and beating each other up. They were the hypocrites.

The priest and deacons from my parents' church would also join us for lunch on Sundays. My father would ask them to bless our god-forsaken house almost weekly. My parents were members of a Catholic/Melkite/ Greek Orthodox Church. They claimed to believe in God but never had a Bible. Believing there is a God is entirely different than having a personal relationship with The God that was willing to give Jesus, His only Son to provide a blood sacrifice for our sins. My parent's sins would have been forgiven – if only they had repented and accepted His free gift of salvation!

Being a church member is often used like "fire insurance." The Bible clearly teaches salvation is by placing faith in Jesus Christ. Jesus said, "I am the way, the truth, and the life: no one comes to the Father except through me." John 14:6

My father's having the priests and deacons continually bless our home was mockery. I believe demons were in and around my entire family.

Food For Thought

A "religious" family doesn't make a good family, but, a father and mother that have a relationship with The Lord and teach their children that relationship – that is what lays the foundation for good family relationships. The family that prays together stays together!

Part 3

Reaping
What We Sow

Detrimental Influences upon My Parents

Just what was it that caused my dad to drink, abuse sex, gamble, and destroy his wife and kids? I think one of the devastating forces in his life was the untimely death of one of my older brothers. Leukemia took the life of my thirteen year old brother at the time I was just a baby. This took a heavy toll on both of my parents, and I am convinced my brother's death contributed to their alcoholism and my dad's abusive nature. I am told my father was so distraught at the funeral that he reached into the casket and tried to take the body out! After cancer took my brother's life, my parents went downhill rapidly, which in turn affected my entire family.

Food For Thought

Things that have an impact on other family members can cause a ripple effect. That effect can be positive – or it can be very negative.

A Ten Year Old Alcoholic

I was a full-blown alcoholic by the age of ten.

There were a number of contributing factors that drove me to drink: **the sexual abuse, the physical abuse, neglect, and emotional abuse.**

Sexual Abuse:

I had been molested on an almost daily basis since the age of six by numerous people.

Physical Abuse:

My father often beat me for my "attitude." He rarely talked with my sister and me, but beating us, though negative, was the most attention we ever got. His only positive interaction, if you could call it that, was when he was drunk... he just didn't know how to love. He would rub his whiskers on my sister and me, to the point of friction burn.

If my sister and I laughed as we tried to joke around before bed, we'd get a razor strap across our legs. I'm not talking about a skinny belt, but a four-inch wide piece of thick leather used to sharpen a razor.

By the time I was six years old, people in my family were offering me sips of alcohol. I'm not suggesting that even a sip is ok, but, the fact is that many sips, one person giving it to you after the other, leads to drunkenness. So who could have been surprised when later, I started drinking at every opportunity?

I would slip downstairs and take whiskey from my father's stashed bottles, replacing what I took with water. He kept his booze in the freezer so it would be cold and whiskey doesn't freeze – that is – unless you add too much water. One day he found his bottle frozen and immediately flew up the stairs and began blaming my mother. When he discovered that it wasn't my mother, he turned to me, and boy did I take a beating!

The Neglect:

My parents would leave us in the hands of mere acquaintances so they could go out to the bars. Most of the time, these people were total strangers to my sister and myself, and we never knew if we could trust them. Most of the time they, too, were out to use and abuse us. Telling my parents would have been redundant, they may have already known, but one way or the other, they didn't seem to care.

Parents are supposed to care for their children, but my parents did not take care of my sister and me. My mom failed to protect us from my dad and did not even comfort us when he was abusive. Never having a momma tuck you in bed at night to comfort you from abuse is very hurtful. It can cause a person to turn inward and to become very withdrawn. It can also cause a person to seek refuge in whatever means available that will help them escape the pain. In my case – I turned to alcohol and eventually prescription valium stolen from my mother.

The Emotional Abuse:

I had no place to escape. I was ridiculed and made fun of by my family and classmates throughout my childhood. My family often called me the "Black Sheep" and the "Troublemaker." My classmates made fun of me because I was slow in school, had hand-me-down boy's clothing, and often fell asleep in class. They also poked fun at me because I was a tom-boy and different. Children should get a good night's rest to be ready for a day of learning when they are going to school, but my house was a party house. Often sleep didn't happen at night. My being tomboy-like was a form of defense. I thought that my abusers would not bother me if I was a boy.

My alcoholic abuse eventually led to anger and suicidal thoughts. By age eleven, I had actually tried to take my own life! I was drinking every day, depressed and unable to concentrate; for these reasons, my parents took me, as well as my baby sister to a psychiatrist. My sister and I suffered with the same issues. The problem was that I couldn't tell the doctor what was wrong. If I had, my dad would have denied the accusation and proceeded to beat me. It was a "catch twenty-two".

Later, I was placed on anti-depressants and sleeping pills. My parents told the doctors that I was so out of control with drinking and drugs that I could not tell the truth. They were right – I could not tell the doctors about my parents and all of the abuse that was taking place in our house!

Alcohol was a way to temporarily numb the pain that I was feeling. I would be intoxicated going to school, but the school never caught on. Since they perceived my family as a "poor family" – they stereotyped me as a lost child who needed to have extra help in reading and counseling, since I repeatedly made failing grades.

I don't know how I managed to pass from one grade to the next. The only class I excelled in was art as it was my way to express myself, so I drew pictures as often as I had a pencil and paper in hand. My daily walk to school was three and a half miles......and I walked because I could not stand being near other kids on the bus. I didn't want to get close to people, because I thought they would not like me. I was broken. I was a drunk. I felt worthless.

Food For Thought

What I didn't know at the time was that there was someone who valued me and saw beyond my brokenness! That Someone was God, and He saw me as priceless....not worthless.

Incest

Our parents often left us alone with one or more of my older brothers. In my opinion – that was a BIG mistake. One of my brothers would beat my little sister and me dragging us across the floor by our hair as if we were little rag dolls, and then he would chase us throughout the house. It took little or nothing to set him off. We often locked ourselves in the bathroom as he raged outside the door. There would be hours of turmoil until he broke down and sobbed, pleading with us for forgiveness.

One of my brothers went way beyond beating. He raped me. I don't remember how it started, but I remember that it happened on a daily basis – even in broad daylight, not just behind closed doors, but even out in the field.

Sometimes this brother would invite his friend to join in on the abuse. He would call him to come along as we would accompany my father to the liquor store. Things would happen right in the backseat of the car – right in my father's presence.

My brother tried to rape one of our neighbors. He took her into a wooden trailer in our backyard. Her brother was in the garden with me. She began screaming, and he released her. I wished that screaming would have caused him to release me – but he never feared what would happen to him because of my screams. Neither my brother, nor my parents were there to come to my rescue.

This same brother got his girlfriend pregnant when he was only fifteen years old. I can remember standing on the back steps and yelling to his girlfriend, "Hey, if it wasn't for me, you would have twenty kids by now!" My dad heard me say that and told me to shut my mouth and get in the house. He **knew** what was happening to me. And at that very second, I knew my father was "allowing" my brother to continuously molest me! I could never depend upon my father for protection. I needed to leave that house even though I was only fourteen. **I needed someone to rescue me!**

Another one of my brothers got out of the military and sodomized me. What he forced upon me was disgusting.

A year or so later, I was asked by another brother to help with a bond fire in our backyard. We were gathering things to pile up to build the fire. As we were pulling old belongings from the garage I saw my old bed frame. (My sister and I had been moved into twin beds.) As I was picking it up, I accidentally dropped the headboard part of the frame. It tipped over, and there I saw dried blood.....it was **my** blood, there because of my head being pounded into the frame when I was being raped repeatedly in that very bed. I still bear the faint scar on my forehead in the shape of a half-moon from that violent experience. That bed was burned that day and part of my own lost soul also seemed to go up in flames with it....I thought burning the bed would make it all go away, but the memory would not burn.

My oldest sister was married. She, too, was a drunk. When she was drunk, she would strip off her top and expose herself to the world. She would kiss me and say that she had heard that lesbians kiss better. That humiliated me so much! She also used to embarrass me at my softball games by showing up in a drunken stupor and running around while wearing no bra.

I don't mean to brag, but I was pretty good at softball. When I came to bat, the other team would walk me in order to prevent a homerun. My sister would yell at the umpires and the other team. She did not know the rules or strategy of the game, and made a fool out of herself.

Perhaps one of the most disgusting things that I remember was when she and my dad made out on the kitchen table. He laid her on the table, right in front of my nephews and nieces, cousins, brothers and sister *and my mom*. My father had the audacity to suggest to my mother that this display was instructional...the way it should be done.

Food For Thought

Who can you trust when you can't trust your own family? There is One (God) who can be trusted.

"There is a friend that sticks closer than a brother." Proverbs 18:24

The Nightmares

You have to remember that I was only around six years old when the sexual abuse started. I began to have frequent nightmares that repeated themselves over and over again until many years later when I finally left home. In my dreams, the walls and ceiling were blacker than black, and blackness was oozing out from the walls and ceiling, having a life of its own. I also had the sensation of falling headlong endlessly.

A snake would come hauntingly toward me, and at times, it was clear that it was not a snake, but rather a very distinct part of male anatomy. I would take this snake in my hands and smash and crush it, breaking it into pieces over and over again, but it would only reform itself, coming back after me night after night.

In other dreams, I was being chased by demons that were covered in blood and gore. They would chase me through parking lots near vehicles, and I would duck in and out of the cars trying to get away and trying to hide under them. But they always found me, and at that point I would awake SO startled!

Food For Thought

Dreams are a tool of the Lord. In order to capture our minds, Satan often mimics the tools of the Lord. Test your dreams and measure them by Scripture. Does the message of your dream match the truth of God's word? (Acts 2:17) Then you can discover the source of your dream.

Why I Became Gay at Ten

I knew I was different at the age of ten when I was attracted to girls my age. I did not like who I was or what I was and didn't understand why I was so different.

The sexual and physical abuse I suffered at the hands of men caused me to be disgusted by men. After what my father had done to me – plus his allowing other men to molest me, the thought of having an intimate relationship with a male caused great fear in me. As a result, I had trouble trusting most people, especially guys! Neglect by my mother and her failure to protect me caused me to seek out someone to fill the void. A mother-child bond is the root of nurturing and social interaction. I now found myself seeking the nurture, love, and care of a mother figure from other women.

Food For Thought

"Two wrongs do not make a right."

It's an old adage, but so very true! God is the only One who can fill the void in your life.

Finally, Mom Takes Action

When the sexual abuse started, mom was complicit with my father's abuse of me, but as time went on, she got sick and tired of my dad abusing me, my baby sister, and her. So, she finally made *some* attempts to rescue all of us from the abuse.

I remember my mom taking my sister and me out of the home in the winter-time so my father wouldn't have his way with us. My older sister's house was our place of refuge from Dad. We all put on our galoshes, I wore my green jacket, while my baby sister put on her blue one and we all trudged through the snow and ice to my older sister's home.

At that time my older sister lived only a half-mile away, and we could get to her house even in heavy snowfall. I remember mom taking us out during a blizzard after they would get home from the bars, because she again was sick and tired of the abuse. I can also remember the four mile walk to my sister's house after she had moved even further from us.

One time Mom got the idea that if she could learn how to drive she could escape the abuse and save us, too. Out of desperation, she asked my dad to give her driving lessons. Dad wasn't fooled by her ploy and guessed her motivation. That first day of lessons was also her final day of driving. He screamed at her so loudly that she never attempted to drive again.

Not only did Dad make Mom scared to approach him about driving, he saw to it that she had no time to leave the house. He bombarded her with work by moving three additional men into the house. He invited his two brothers and a black man that he had met at a bar to live with us. She basically became a servant for these men.

My mom was getting older, and all of a sudden she was taking on more responsibility instead of slowing down. She cooked all the meals, washed and folded all the clothes, cleaned the house. She was a maid. It was incredible what she endured, all just so my father could keep her from leaving with us kids. She was trapped with no way out.

Food For Thought

I experienced a mix of emotions as I watched someone who was partially to blame for my abuse, being abused herself. I believe this may have been the beginning of empathy (and forgiveness later) on my part, as I associated myself with my mother's hurt.

Part 4

Self Destruction

Falsely Accused

Again, when I was about twelve years old, my parents took me to a mental health center along with my baby sister for analysis and counseling. That would have been a perfect opportunity for us to tell the authorities what was happening, but tragically, I felt I could say nothing because my accusers were in the same room. My Dad and Mom both said we were bad kids, and Mom actually walked out during the session in tears because she claimed we treated her so poorly. You know, I don't ever remember treating her badly. I don't remember back-talking to her, but I do remember feeling badly for the things that she had to endure at the hand of my dad.

My parents were the problem – not my sister and I. I wish my mom would have gotten counseling. She could possibly have been able to expose the problems that the whole family was enduring. Instead, from fear, she lied to protect my father.

It is tragic that the mental health center did not pick up on the fact that something was wrong. The counselor could have met with my sister and me alone to get our side of the story, but neglected to do so. I honestly don't know if either of us would have had the courage to report the abuse to the counselor had she met privately with us, but we never had that opportunity. As a result, the suffering and abuse continued.

Food For Thought

I was accused of being bad. I honestly do not remember being bad. I do remember that I wanted to scream. I wanted to scream so loudly that someone would come to our rescue. What I didn't realize was that Someone WAS listening...even to my silent cries.

A Failed Attempt to Escape
Through Suicide

After I started drinking more heavily and taking more of mother's valium, I turned also to marijuana and other street drugs. *My mother was taking valium which the doctor had prescribed as a sedative to eradicate her depression. Someone should have told him that two downers don't make a pick-me-up.* I also started cutting myself....the cutting was pain that I could control...and it was a release.

The turmoil in my life was so bad that I wanted to end it all. I did not want to be like my parents, but in some ways I was **just like them** – a drunk – dysfunctional – an abuser with no self-worth. My soul was sinking to what was an endless... never-ending.... dark pit of hell and rage. **I wanted out.**

One afternoon I started drinking and hung rope from the rafter of the garage. I had it all planned. I continued drinking and used red paint to cover the exposed beams for I wanted to symbolize how much I was bleeding and hurting on the inside... but before I could hang myself, I was so drunk that I passed out! My brother and father found me on the floor of the garage later that afternoon. I woke up confused and surprised that I was still alive, **but I sure didn't want to be!**

Food For Thought

Abuse is a vicious cycle. I did not choose to be abused, but, as so often is the case with others, I found myself being abused at my own hand. The abusive cycle seems to have no end – but it does in fact have a cure...it is found in the Lord.

Working My Anger Out

I had failed at attempted suicide, and though the anger increased, life continued for me. Leather straps and getting raped over and over again will tend to enrage a person. I wanted to hurt the people who caused me to feel all that pain, but I dared not. So, in order to work out the anger I worked hard at manual labor, tilling gardens and shoveling dirt. I had four large gardens that I tended and worked with my brother cutting log pieces and hauling them for cord wood. I also had a paper route of over 100 papers to deliver 7 days a week, and not having a bike, I was carrying everything on foot. I was often bitten by dogs as I placed the papers in the doorways. I was often exposed to the dirty old men in the neighborhood that seemed to have nothing better to do than expose themselves to a hard working young girl. My father wanted my baby sister to deliver papers, as well, but one of my brothers jumped to her defense. He knew what I had to face on my route.

This work was therapy for me, because I was able to get my mind off of failing grades at school and problems at home. I would work to the point of exhaustion, and it felt good to get the anger out of my system. The hard work was much more therapeutic than drowning myself with alcohol. Unfortunately, the therapy would only last during the day, because I had to return home to the house that was the source of my anger.

I **dreaded** going home. There were times that I would catch a glimpse into a family that seemed so normal and happy. So many times, I came close to telling someone about the abuse, thinking they might be able to help, but, I didn't want to upset those happy families. Then they would have needed to get involved in my family's affairs.

Therapy was all that I got from the jobs I worked. My father kept all the money that I received from the paper route, but I did spend a nickel on a pack of peanuts once. I thought I had hidden the wrapper, and when he found it – the consequences were not pretty.

I found another source of release in playing softball. However, I didn't hang out with the team outside of the game because I didn't want them to get to know me and find out what my family was like. I played any position on the field and I most often hit a homerun when I took the bat. I received MVP awards, yet, I never felt I measured up. I didn't drink as much then, but I still would carry alcohol with me onto the field as my "security".

Food For Thought

I reached a point that I thought my life had no worth and I actually tried to end it. However, God knew the plans He had for me and stopped me.

Part 5

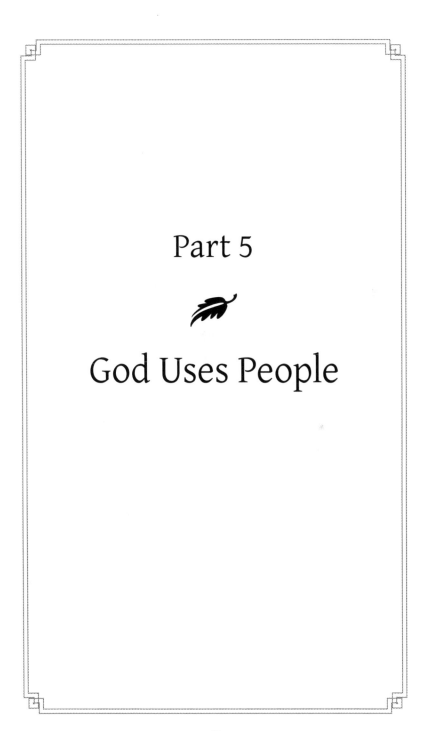

God Uses People

Caring Teachers

When I was in junior high school I met a great art teacher. He had what he called "a love rug" that the kids all sat on in class and shared how we were feeling. One of our class assignments was to write a couple of sentences about how we were feeling that particular day.

I wrote, "I am sad, because, if the kids knew me they would not like me, and if they knew what was happening at my home, they would never talk to me." Out of twenty-five children in my class, he figured out it was me who wrote those sentences. He asked me to stay after class and talk with him. For some reason, I did not feel threatened by this kind teacher.

He later asked and received my parent's permission to pick me up for ice cream on Saturdays. We had a great time doing that for months. I didn't look at him as most young girls might, with a crush, but rather in my eyes – this man was a perfect father.

He had such a kind heart and was always willing to listen to me share what was happening in my family. In retrospect, I believe he was a Christian and prayed for me, which is the best thing he could have done. He so encouraged me and I believe he would have taken me away from the abuse if he could have. I never really told him everything that was happening, and shared only nuggets and tidbits of my life circumstances. I feared that if he knew everything that was going on, his life would be in jeopardy just as mine was.

My parents became jealous of this teacher and accused me of having an affair with him. My brothers were told about him, and they questioned me about what was going on. My father sat me down and told me to tell him to stop coming around – I was so upset. Reacting out of fear, I told my teacher that he couldn't come back. The following year, I started high school and I still miss this precious teacher who has since passed on. I expect to run into him again someday in Heaven and perhaps have the opportunity to thank him for the contribution he made to my life.

At some point, around the age of fourteen, I became a determined person. I wanted to be somebody important to someone and not the person that was shaped by abuse.

Later, my science teacher at school became involved and I believe she was a Christian, too. I just happened to be on the phone with her one day while my mom and dad were fighting. I didn't realize that she could hear what was going on in the background, but she overheard Mom say to Dad, "If you want to have sex, have it with your daughter because I am not having sex with you anymore!" I was shocked when she asked if she had heard what she thought she had heard. She said, "I am coming to get you," and I agreed for her to do so.

She came right over and got me and took me out of the house. She tried talking to my parents, but they actually told her it was none of her business! Her attempt to help changed nothing.

One day I came home from school and was ready to end my life. I was taking drugs for depression but they were not helping – they may have even been contributing to the problem.

This teacher saw that I was having a rough day and gave me a ride home from school. She didn't just drop me off that day, but came in and ended up sitting up with me all night long to keep me from hurting myself. She hadn't eaten before we came home, and she didn't eat all night. Instead of being appreciative for her intervention, my mother was accusatory. Wondering "what kind of teacher would do this kind of thing" – she thought she had some warped motive. My mother had no idea that if this teacher had not intervened, I would probably have taken my life that night!

I began attending prayer meetings with my teacher at her church, and she and her friends actually prayed over me. I was hearing them talk "about God" and "to God." I even went through the motions of praying myself. I realized that there was a big void in my life that needed to be filled. I wanted to be loved and not abused. What I thought I needed was another human to fill that void and love me. This science teacher was helping me with my school work, but she was helping me with so much more. She had a relationship with God, and I now believe that God was drawing me to Himself through the power of her prayers.

I was grieved over the fact that my family and friends didn't truly care about me, but as I spent time with people from this church I began to entertain the idea that "maybe" God really did care about me. I was so tired of being trapped in the life I was living – I still wanted out and I still wanted to die. It was hard for me to sleep, hard to eat, and very hard to concentrate.

I would sit in my closet, writing and drawing on the walls. I had questions about why the God that I was hearing about would allow me to be used the way I was being used. This place called Hell, this place of torment that was described in the church… I felt as if that was what my house was like. I felt like I was going mad, and I was going to snap and never be able to come back.

Food For Thought

Things were bad in the house where I lived and I had a difficult time calling it "home". I did realize there were "outside" people who cared and tried to help me, and I looked forward to spending time with them.

"God, Show Me You Are Real."

One day I actually cried out to God. I asked Him "if He was real" to give me some kind of "sign", but my dad interrupted me and told me to help him bring in the groceries. So – I left my bedroom to help him and when I came back in my room, my record player was on!!! The arm was down, the record was revolving, but the needle was not advancing, and no music was coming from it. It was as though it were stuck in a groove. "I" did not turn it on, and there was no one else there to have turned it on. This was my first sense that God was real. My sense was the God they talked about in church had turned on my record player! He had given me the sign, just as I had asked.

Even later that same day, I questioned whether something I had done had caused the record player to turn on. I believed something unique had happened, but I still had my doubts about God.

Food For Thought

"But God demonstrates his own love for us in this: While we were still sinners, Christ died for us." Romans 5:8 Even when I only knew of the existence of God, He was placing people in my life to teach me about Him. I was not there yet, but God was wooing me into a personal relationship with Him.

Part 6

Separating From Family

Running, But Not Far Enough

I tried running away from home when I was fourteen, only to be brought back home by the police. Upon my return, my parents told me that they had talked to a man from the local detention center for troubled kids. They threatened that if I tried to escape again I could be locked up in the center. Ironically, the man from the detention center (whom they just happened to meet at the bar!) was allowed to move into our home. My father had found places for the other men to live, but here again was someone for my mom to serve. He had a large key ring to the center's cell doors with 50 to 100 keys on it. He would often shake the ring of keys at me and say, "I will lock you up and throw away the key and you'll never be able to come back here!" Talk about more abuse!

Food For Thought

Abuse takes on many faces. It comes from many directions. Emotional abuse hurts just as bad as, or worse than physical abuse. Internal scars are just as real as external ones.

The Final Straw That Caused Me to Leave Home

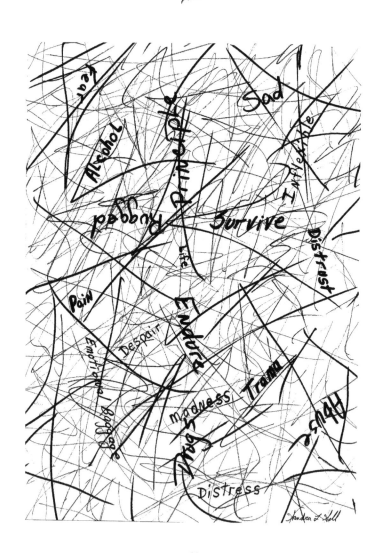

My drinking continued and worsened. I would drink so much that I often threw up. Alcohol poisoning was nothing unusual for me, and the hospital was a common stop. I would also blackout from drinking and not remember where I had been or what I was doing.

I was driving illegally at fifteen, stealing my father's car and trying to get away. One night I stuffed pillows in my bed, slipped out and took his car. He awakened and noticed that the car was gone! He began checking to see who might be missing in the house to determine who could have taken it. When he thought everyone was accounted for, he called the police. They found the car and me in it. A high-speed chase ensued, and I hit the guard rail at about 80 mph coming off the ramp. I didn't care. I just wanted out.

The police cuffed me and took me into the Police Department. My sister and father came and got me, and of course, they told the officers how "bad" I was. They discussed putting me in a juvenile detention center, and when it was my turn to speak, I told the officers that I wanted to leave home. My sister was taunting me that I wasn't going to have to worry about going home, because I was going to the detention center since I was causing my parents nothing but pain. *Not one word was mentioned of the pain that they were causing me!* The officers told me that if I could get a job and support myself, that I could leave home!

My mother had been taking spells of chasing us around the house with knives for several years. She never cut us, but the threat was always present. She seemed to always be flipped-out on valium and alcohol. I can still see her blood-red face screaming at us. The neighbors came to our aid on more than one occasion and bound her hands and feet, tying her to a chair. My dad had driven her nearly to the point of insanity. But, he was a popular guy in the community, and the neighbors thought that they were doing the right thing by detaining her until he came home and took over.

I had to stay in the home until getting employment, so Mom and I often talked about where I could possibly work. Months later, my parents had realized that I was growing stronger in my determination to get away from the abuse, so they took me to a psychologist to get some medication to calm me down. My parents gave him their side of the story and then I tried to talk to him, and actually opened up to him more than I had to probably anyone else. However, I was still afraid to go into details of the abuse from men. I was too embarrassed to tell him about the countless violations from men in my own home!

During the confidential sessions, I did, however, confide in him about my attraction towards females and expressed being perplexed about the attraction.

The outcome of the doctor visits was his telling my parents that I was gay and would be for the rest of my life. **I did not want that diagnosis; I just wanted him to "fix" me!** *At this point in my life I had experienced no gay relationship. I thought I was different – I was embarrassed to shower with other girls in gym class. I did indeed desire the affection of a female, namely my mother, and I did* **not** *desire affection from men. I didn't know what my problem was or how to describe it to anyone else.* His "prescription" was a note to the school saying that it was best for me to leave school and go to work.

From that point on my whole family began calling me "Lizzy." They were vicious with their criticism.

Our house was indeed a house of horrors!

The abuse had gotten worse. It only took the smallest thing to set my father off. At the least, my father would beat me about the face as he knelt on my shoulder so I could not move. One day I was on the phone looking for a job while one of my brothers was at the house drinking with my dad. The more they drank, the worse they wanted me to get off the phone. No one needed the phone – they just wanted me to get **off** the phone. I got so upset that I finally flipped and pulled the phone cord out of the wall. That was it for my dad – he started shoving me and slapping me in the face. I tried to push him away, but my drunken brother joined in and helped my father hold me down and beat me. (From that episode I had a blood blister on my lower lip that took about eleven years to go away.) **That was the last straw! I had had enough! One way or the other I was going to get out of that house!** At this point, I could not even trust my sibling to protect me….after all, it was just a silly phone cord which I later fixed.

My doctor was right on target about me needing to work – school was not the place for me. The therapeutic benefits of working hard made work the only logical choice at that time.

I could not handle being around school kids of my own age. I had nothing in common with them, especially since they had let me know I was an outcast, often ridiculing me. I had become so embittered toward them through the years for their taunting me, and it only accentuated my feelings of insecurity. I also felt something was wrong with me sexually, but at that time, I didn't understand what it was exactly or why I had become that way….I just knew I was different!

My doctor saw that work was beneficial to my health, because when I worked or played hard it seemed to drain the anger out of me, at least temporarily. He had observed that I kept my sanity by playing softball, drawing, walking everywhere I went, and working hard. I still had my old familiar crutches, alcohol and drugs, which were used less than before at this point in time.

My parents calling me a "Lizzy" and letting everyone in my family know what the doctor had said was a final straw. They all made fun of me, accusing me of bringing shame to the family. It was more than I could stand. They, who were drunkards, abusers, and deceivers, were putting the burden of shame on me. For so long, I had tolerated the brunt of their abuse and never told anyone! My situation had been forced upon me by their actions and I was trapped! To them, I was the "troublemaker" and the "black sheep of the family," causing problems. I drank and did drugs just like they did – they are the ones who fed me the alcohol leading to addiction! It made no sense to me!!! **What I did know was – I was getting out!**

Finally, I got a job and went to live with my brother and his family, and that is when the nightmares ended. My job situation was ideal because my brother and I worked almost side by side of each other.

I thought my brother had rescued me, but it only lasted a few months. Unfortunately, I soon realized he and his wife were not getting along, so within just a few months I had to go back to my parents' home.

Food For Thought

It's incredible the way that others can mold and shape us. A perfectly normal person can be made to believe that "he" or "she" alone is the problem, while all along the problems are being mostly created, provoked, and maintained by others.

Moving Farther Away
From My Childhood

I had no intention of remaining in that house. I had experienced a taste of freedom and was determined to get away again as soon as possible. I ran into a lady that I had recently worked with, and she and her husband were willing to take me into their home. She was thirty-five years older than me, as old as my mom.

I took a huge step and moved away from my family after having been sexually abused on an almost daily basis for all those years. Leaving the house did not eliminate the anguish within me. Part of me felt that I was leaving my mother to the wolves and I felt sorry for her. Ours was a love-hate relationship. I was so torn apart, and the pain within me was so deep that I was turning to any feel-good drug I could get. I was drinking and drugging to not only bury the past, but also to cope with the burdens I was presently carrying in my life. I had been labeled a "black sheep" and "troublemaker." Now, my parents said I had broken their hearts by moving out. My mother said I had replaced her with another mother, and I now believe she was right. Mother was never really there for me when I needed her, and I believe I truly did search for someone to fill that void.

This woman ended up being my first gay encounter. I thought she and her husband were attempting to rescue me from my family. She had won my trust. As I shared the ugliness of my abuse with her, I reached out to her for comfort. One thing led to another, and eventually her comfort became something indecent. Her husband also became inappropriate. **I thought I had escaped, but I had only changed households.** Looking for relief, I continued drinking and doing drugs and again, I tried to kill myself. Much of this move is a blur, because I had gotten into hallucinogenic drugs. It's a wonder that I lived!

Food For Thought

As they say, "out of the frying pan and into the fire." Searching for answers can lead to a resolution for a problem – but, deception can play a huge role and create even more problems. If I had only known then what I know now…that, everything that happened in my life happened for a reason. It has taken every single building block, rough as they may have been at the time, to make me who I am today.

Part 7

Raw Emotional Pain

My Brother's Motorcycle Accident

I remained in that house with this friend and her husband for a couple of years and then moved to another town to live with a niece of theirs.

In the new place, an apartment, there was a phone jack, but no phone. I remember one evening I kept going to where the telephone was supposed to be. I was restless and could not sleep and was sick to my stomach. I kept feeling like I should call my parents, but we didn't have a phone.

I now believe that this was premonition. I don't know the source of the warning. What I know is that I felt that night like part of me was dying. I was on edge. I was crying. It was just all very strange.

The next day was May 19th. I had been listening to the radio and doing laundry when my baby sister and sister-in-law came to my door. They had driven twenty-five miles to come see me and when I opened the door, I saw that they were upset and crying. They told me that my brother had been in a bad accident. My parents had sent them to bring me home.

On the ride back we actually joked about being so low on gasoline that we might not make it back home. . We were laughing in a time of crisis – my brother had survived accidents before and I had no reason to believe that he would not pull through this time. *I was soon to find that I was the only one in the car with what I believed was reason to hope – they already knew.*

As we pulled into the neighborhood there was a commotion, and the policemen were directing traffic. My oldest brother, the one that had been so abusive to me, met me at the sidewalk and told me that our brother was dead. It took me very little time to let him know that I wished it had been him instead. And then, I went into shock. I only have bits and pieces of memory from the following days. I doubt that many in the household remember very much, since they were all drinking and taking prescription drugs.

I had great difficulty accepting my brother's death. I was so distraught that I didn't attend his funeral. I had nightmares that he was calling me from a telephone in the cemetery. He was asking me, "Why didn't you come to say goodbye to me?"

According to my family, the director of the funeral home said that my brother's funeral service was the largest they had ever seen. For years after his death, I coped by telling myself he had gone back into the Air Force. I used to visit his gravesite regularly. I would sit, cry, drink alcohol, and do drugs until I fell asleep on his grave.

This was the second son that my parents had lost. Before this brother died, he was struggling with living and was also in the process of getting a divorce. He had been drinking with my family the night before he was cut off on the roadway and died as a result of his motorcycle crash.

I know the abuse and the hurts that had happened to me, but I don't know all of what may or may not have happened to my older brothers and sisters before me. I don't know exactly what caused my father to be so abusive and I have often thought he must have been reared in an abusive environment himself. I do know that his actions were passed on to my brothers who became abusive themselves. In the midst of everything, I felt a strong obligation to protect my baby sister.

A few years later, I went to a rehabilitation home where I made several really good friends. There was one lady and her family who invited me to their home to share meals with them. After several months of friendship – one night out of the blue, she shared – to my shock – that it was her father that had killed my brother in the accident. **It was an accident!** "Forgiveness" was becoming a word in my vocabulary.

Food For Thought

Abuse tends to be a vicious cycle, one that takes an incredible act to break. Forgiveness breaks the cycle.

My First Tattoo

In my early twenties, I had my first tattoo put on my left arm. At this point, I was a mess. I had reached my lowest point to date. I had made two really bad choices in a short time and was actually looking at jail time for pursuing money for drugs. I was seeking freedom, and in retrospect – believe that God was pursuing me.

I certainly was not a Christian at the time, but, it is important to remember that I had been around people who were Christians. I had been to church and sat under their teaching and knew a bit about talking the talk, but I wasn't "walking the walk" of a true believer.

So – one afternoon when I was feeling particularly alone, I opened up the Bible. Whatever verse I happened to read at that time seemed to point me to the crown of thorns and thoughts of repentance. I have no idea why, but found myself in a tattoo shop with the crown of thorns painfully being applied to my left forearm.

The thoughts of anger and pain in my heart were unrelenting. Getting one tattoo was not enough – it was only the beginning and eight more followed. Some of them I did myself! Inking is painful, and so self-inflicted inking is like cutting – it is self-mutilation. Why in the world would someone do this? The answer: it is pain for pain. I wanted to confront my parents at that time, but I couldn't build up the courage to do so. I was still afraid of them, yet I was still seeking love and attention from my parents. I desperately wanted to release all my mental, emotional, and physical pain and found at least one sure thing – tattoos did not work!

Food For Thought

Putting tattoos on your body is something that is pretty much permanent. They can be removed, but it is costly and actually a bit dangerous. The scarring from the lasers can be as bad as a third degree burn. What's there is outward, and depending on placement, usually visible. All the while that I was creating these outward markings, I was dealing with turmoil within. The scars that are left on the inside are just as bad as, or worse than the ones on the outside. Funny thing – you would think that inner scars are hidden from view, but they sometimes show worse than the outer ones. People do judge a book by its cover. Seldom do people look into the pages to understand a person's full story.

Part 8

Doing Things
On My Own

A Clear Mind Seeking God's Presence

Having tried to rehabilitate myself a couple of times before, and finding self-help rarely worked, I checked myself into a rehab center for drugs and alcohol. This time I had hit rock bottom, and it seemed like the devil was waiting to shovel the dirt on top of me. I entered into an in-patient program for people who had mental health issues due to drug addiction.

The rehabilitation program turned out to be a temporary success for me and I managed to achieve one year of sobriety taking no street drugs. Living in the center allowed me to be constantly involved in Narcotics Anonymous and Alcoholics Anonymous. Beginning at 5:30 am and going until 10pm, I attended as many as forty meetings a week.

It was while I was in this rehab program that the concept of "a power greater than me," being in control of my life and having the potential to "restore me back to sanity," was introduced. Many of the people in the program referred to their "higher power" without referring to God. I, on the other hand, believed in God and recognized Him as being *"The" Higher Power.* I could see Him as being the One in control, the One that had kept me from destruction.

My parents had taught me a concept of God, and had actually taken me to church. I had also attended church with one of my teachers and heard about Him there. So, this "higher power" that was being talked about was not a foreign concept to me.

People in these meetings often talked about having some sort of "spiritual awakening," and I wanted to have this kind of experience. One early morning about 6 am, I went to the lake to read the Bible as this had become a regular practice for me. I had hoped that something within the pages of that book would prompt a spectacular event for me, this "spiritual awakening" that I so desired.

Sitting there in my truck, looking out over the lake, I fell asleep reading. When I woke up I had the Bible clutched to my chest. I was fully awake. There were some guys that pulled alongside of me and unloaded a canoe into the water. I could see the fog lying just above and beyond a patch of water-lilies. There was a blue heron standing just in front of the lilies on a boulder and behind the fog, there were *misty white things* – things that I could see through, but they had a shape. They were descending on the left side, dancing across the water and afterward ascending up into the sun. I watched for twenty minutes – there was no rush and mind you, I was sober and drug-free, so I was not hallucinating!

When the fog lifted – they were gone but the blue heron was still there, and the guys that had launched the canoe were visible off in the distance. I was excited!!! I had my longed for "spiritual awakening," for which I had prayed. I returned to the rehab house and shared what I had seen. Some of those that I shared with were pleased and supportive, others were skeptical.

At this point, reader, I want to make it very clear that this experience, as I later realized, was not the ultimate salvation experience with God, my *Higher Power*. However, through this experience at the lake, He did prove He was present and actively, lovingly, pursuing a personal relationship with me.

Food For Thought

Admitting a problem is the first step to recovery, but there are many steps that follow. There are not necessarily "12 Steps." The most important steps lead to the recognition of a need for a Savior and the establishment of a relationship with Him. God's Spirit was drawing me. There was more to come.

Relapse

After thirteen months of sobriety, I left the rehab program. The staff at the center pleaded with me not to go. I was healing, but I was far from well. I was being drawn by God's Holy Spirit, but I had not repented and had not established a relationship with the Lord. I was not strong enough to stand against the temptations. When I became involved with someone whose lifestyle involved alcohol, I fell right back into my old ways. You cannot run with bad company and expect to not sin.

Depression, sadness, and loneliness were knocking at my door again. I was back into alcohol, drugs, sex, and gambling. Once more, I was so low. Again, I tried suicide…this time by carbon monoxide poisoning in my garage. I should have died, but I didn't. After being rescued by family members, my brother asked me, "Teri, why did you do it?" My answer was, **"I am tired of hurting, and I don't want to live like this anymore!"** God had spared me once again!

Afterwards, I was hospitalized in a psychiatric hospital and while there, I had a very vivid flashback of an extremely violent rape at the hands of one of my brothers. In the dream, I was only about ten years old and was being sodomized repeatedly. I fought to wake up, but the dream seemed to last forever. When I finally did awaken, I called upon the staff members at the hospital to help me deal with this nightmare. Their conclusion was that I was bipolar with manic episodes.

You can imagine that my prior dealings with doctors had caused me to mistrust the medical profession. They had written me off as "gay forever" and fed me sleeping pills and anti-depressants. My counselors at the mental health center had sided with my parents' version of my behavior. They prescribed medications like everyone before – so – with good reasons, I developed a healthy mistrust of doctors. Instead of getting to the root of the problem, they threw medicine at me! **This was no fix.** It actually worsened my condition, causing me to draw further inward!

I was in my mid-twenties, and by this time I had been out of my parents' home for several years, but they were still called in to consult with the doctors. Mom and Dad seemed to be more concerned about the other patients and why they were in the hospital, than they were with me. They had nothing to offer in the way of helping me.

I remained at the hospital for ten days and completed a portion of the life skills program. When I left, they gave me lots of materials on alcoholism, drug addiction, and manic depression. I tried to share some of the materials with my parents, but they insisted that they had no need of such and told me to stop coming around. They continued with the same lifestyle they lived during my growing up years. I knew that I could not be around that way of life – so staying away was not a problem for me!

Food For Thought

There's an old saying "when you lie down with dogs, you get up with fleas." Leaving rehab and getting into a relationship with someone that was as broken as I was, was a mistake!

"Blessed is the one who does not walk in step with the wicked or stand in the way that sinners take or sit in the company of mockers." Psalm 1:1

Part 9

Debilitating Health

One Illness after Another

Since 1989 I have had 12 operations, including 3 back surgeries (the last one through my abdomen). The last of those back surgeries was in 1998, and for about a year I was in a brace which locked my right leg in place and made it extremely hard to move around.

At the time, I was living with a girlfriend. We were together as a couple for a year, but later became just best of drinking buddies. She was a nurse and a great caregiver.

I was still a very angry person and was also feeling useless and bitter at being disabled.

This friend and I had purchased a house together. While I was healing from the surgery I poured myself into unbelievably hard work to fix the place up.

Eventually, I stopped drinking (surprisingly, overnight!), and it's a good thing. God gets the glory, because He did it! It had never bothered me previously to drink and take pills at the same time. At this juncture, I was taking 1,200 pills per month, prescribed by four different doctors for fourteen years of my pitiful life.

Prescriptions were from the orthopedic surgeon, a pain management doctor, a neurologist, a cardiologist, and a psychologist. For breakfast, I had a cup of coffee with 25 pills. There were days that I literally had to set my alarm to take the dogs out. I had pills to wake up, pills to put me to sleep, pills for before meals, and pills for after meals. In one year's time, I filled a 50 gallon trash bag with empty medicine bottles. I had gone from being a drunkard to being a prescription drug addict. I was not abusing the drugs – the drugs were abusing me. I became a person that was not very easy to be around. I hurt the people that I was around, especially my best friend. For this reason, I found myself apologizing often for my attitude.

Eventually, my friend confronted the doctor about the amount of medication I was taking and what it was doing to me. He strongly objected, citing scientific studies proving why he had me on the meds. She was concerned the meds were going to kill me! The doctor pretty much told her to mind her own business!

I went to my primary care physician, and he weaned me off of some meds, while at the same time, I began to search for holistic ways to be healed.

In 2004 I faced a new battle – this time it was potential lung cancer. In 2007 I had a heart attack and after that, I had a complete hysterectomy and multiple-hernia operations. I developed severe infections due to the lack of sterilization following the last surgery. I was in the operating room twice in nine days for the same procedure. I had to return to the Emergency Room five times and was admitted to the hospital three out of those five times.

After forty-five injections, drawing blood and running intravenous fluids, the nurses finally just went main-line through my jugular vein. I was put on a high protein diet and given steroids because of the infections. As a result, I gained over 125 pounds and was told that the doctors suspected that I had cancer and diabetes.

As a result of the infections, my body did not heal quickly from the surgery and I had an open wound for eight months. Nurses had to change the dressing for the wound three times a day. I had a KCI vacuum system hooked into my abdomen sucking out all the infections. To this day my abdomen is deformed.

Food For Thought

Abuse takes a heavy toll on a person's mind and body. Not all of my abuse had been external; much of it was self-inflicted and penetrated deep into my emotions. Doctors could not reach the depth of my problems. My need required a touch from the Great Physician. My healing was yet to come.

My Lengthy Battle with Health

In 2004 my doctor told me I might have lung cancer, because there was a big spot on my left lung. I had to have a PET scan to clarify if it was cancer and to determine what type, yet the scan was not conclusive. Further testing revealed that my lung was encompassed with a bacterial mold. I lived that way for about a year – the pain was horrific.

Surgery to break the encapsulation of mold away – which was debilitating for me, was the only solution to the problem. The surgeon had to actually massage the bottom lobe of my lung to try to get it to work again. I was told what should have been about the size of a grapefruit was only about the size of a walnut. What they had anticipated to be a one and a half hour surgery ended up taking six and a half hours! They even had to administer a second epidural.

I was being administered a synthetic heroin. I was in so much pain and on so many other drugs that I scarcely knew my own name. **I begged for them to just kill me!**

From there, I had to go to the Center for Disease Control in order to prevent infection. I was told I would have to return to the hospital for an additional fourteen days and be placed on experimental drugs to get rid of the mold and bacteria that was still in and around my left lung. I had become somewhat of a human guinea pig.

Instead of yielding to the experimentation, I chose to leave my life in God's hands, believing He would see me through it all. It's important to note that, at that time, I did not fully understand Biblical teaching about a true faith relationship with Jesus, the Savior. Somehow though, with my limited understanding, I had enough faith in God to trust Him with my life and for recovery from lung cancer. I did survive. All the while, God was increasing my faith and understanding of His power.

Soon after I left the CDC, severe depression set in. I thought I had known depression for years, but this was major depression. **It was a nightmare.** No matter what I did, nothing was working anymore. I had the mouth of a sailor and I was angry, tired, lonely, and wanted it all just to stop.

One evening, I took out my painter's easel and a canvas and picked up my paint brush. Placing it in the black paint, I started painting a picture of a woman with long wavy hair, thick eyebrows, wide forehead, beautiful teeth, and an oval face, with hazel eyes. I didn't have a model. I had never met the woman I was painting. I started getting confused, and asked God, "Why am I painting this woman?" I received no answer. Perhaps I received no answer, because this picture was not from God!

Frustration came over me, and I then proceeded to cover the picture in figure eights.

I put the painting aside on the floor in the corner of the room, and then I moved it to another room and put it in a chair for a few days. There was something just gnawing at me. I couldn't figure out why I had covered the portrait in figure eights.

As I researched the meaning of the figure eight symbol, I found that it meant *infinity*. It reminded me of the fact that I had been seeking for God to send me a soul mate that would be with me forever. At the time, the image of that mate was based on the fact that I had been convinced that I had been born gay. I had been specifically praying to God to send someone to me for that purpose, and was on the "look out" for someone special. Mind you, I was still living in my own home, with my best friend and caregiver, while searching for a meaningful, intimate relationship. At this home, I had a measure of financial security and a dependable companion.

My looking got me into trouble, because I moved in with someone, only knowing her for a couple of weeks. I was so determined to find someone that would love me that I allowed myself to become entrapped again by another abusive relationship which may well have been the worst yet, for I was constantly looking over my shoulder and made to feel like nothing that I did was right. It wasn't long until my weak body rebelled with a heart attack.

I got up one morning and was so sick. Still I followed through with a promise to go grocery shopping for my sister. I made it through the store, but was sick to my stomach in the parking lot. I knew that there was something wrong and even suspected that it might be a heart attack, but didn't want to overreact. I took the groceries to my sister's home and sat in the air-conditioned room, but the pain would not go away. Finally, after a full day of battling the pain, I called the ambulance.

By the time that the EMTs arrived, my partner had also arrived. I wanted out of the abusive situation, but I was so fearful. I really felt that the stress of the relationship was a contributing factor to my current pain. Even the emergency responders questioned me about my safety. They could see that there was a problem with the relationship.

On that very day I stopped smoking. I finished my cigarette before they put me in the ambulance, and that was the last one I ever smoked. I was that scared that I was going to die.

At the hospital, I remained conscious. My blood pressure was skyrocketing, but the doctor wasn't convinced I was having a heart attack. It wasn't until sixteen hours later that the tests confirmed that I had passed a blood clot through my heart.

Prior to my heart attack, my brother had urged me to end the destructive relationship with my latest partner. I took his counsel, despite her begging me to come back home. When I left the hospital I was given the opportunity to go to my brother's to stay and needless to say – I took him up on it!

Remember the painting I had set aside after being perplexed? While I was recovering from the heart attack, I met the spitting-image of the female that I had painted, which I will call Delilah, and we dated for three years. It too was a financially draining and needy relationship.

I can't explain how or why the Lord was working with me, but I believe He was using each event of my life as a stepping stone on a path toward Him – each step compelling me to a relationship with Him.

It didn't take long for me to see that *my* perfect image was not what God had planned for me. I began to see that *my* choice for a life mate was not as perfect as I had anticipated. There was something more that I was seeking.

Food For Thought

Hebrews 4:12 says, "For the word of God is alive and active. Sharper than any double-edged sword, it penetrates even to dividing soul and spirit, joints and marrow; it judges the thoughts and attitudes of the heart." Jesus, (John 14:8) was at work in my heart – molding and changing me – drawing me into a relationship with Him that was to transcend all my expectations of the perfect soul-mate.

Saved from Suicide by God's Intervention

While still in the dating relationship with the woman of the painting, I fell into the deepest depression of my life. I really and truly wanted to die. I didn't want to answer the phone or talk to anyone. I started getting my house in order, so as not to leave a mess for others.

This had been a while in coming, for suicide had been brewing in the back of my mind. After a week's preparation, I knew I had reached the end of my rope. I lined up 14 bottles of prescription drugs, and I started a letter to my non-existent family – however I never completed it. Throughout the course of the day and night as I glanced at those bottles, I knew that if I did what I was contemplating, my life would end forever.

My tears seemed endless – I couldn't believe my life had come to this. I was so sick of being sick all the time, and at the whims of the doctors and medical professionals. I cried out to God that evening. It seemed that I always found myself turning toward God as a last resort, but, I had never literally cried out to him... this was totally different.

So, on my knees, I said, "God, if you don't help me, I am going to hell!" – I somberly got into bed. As I lowered my head on the pillow, I saw Satan in the form of the Grim Reaper standing right in front of me with his sickle.

He then swooped under my bed, and I knew he was waiting for me.

The next morning as I woke, I heard a very real whisper in my right ear that said, **"life style change"**. I now believe that it was God speaking to me. I had called upon the Lord and He had answered me! This was a totally new concept for me. I thought I had everything worked out in my mind about how things should be, and here He was telling me to change everything. **He was telling me to "live" and not die.** On top of that, He said to change my lifestyle. How could I do that after 40 years of living the same way?! After all, I was born that way!

I cannot fully explain everything that happened in that moment and in the days that followed. But, I believe this was my conversion experience. I truly trusted the Savior, Jesus, with my life.

From this point, I was willing to be different. I was supposed to make a lifestyle change? I thought, "Okay, I'll do it." So, I quit all the medications overnight. I should have died from the withdrawals, but I didn't. Morphine, valium, oxycodone, seizure meds, pills for my heart and blood pressure, nitro glycerin, pills to wake me up, pills to put me to sleep, and pills for my mood swings were all there one day and gone the next!

Food For Thought

So often we think we are in charge of our lives. Learning that we are not the author of our own destiny is a very important lesson. I was trying to orchestrate my own life. For me, finally yielding to God's leadership and authority lifted my incredible

heavy burden! *In fact that "burden" was lifted two thousand years ago, and nailed to a cross, covered in the blood of the only begotten Son of God on Calvary. Who is carrying your burden?*

Part 10

A Clear Message

"Dust Your Feet at the Door"

After stopping all my meds "cold turkey," I had thought, "What now?" I heard the prompting to make a lifestyle change – but, I still didn't know what all that entailed.

I, relying on my own volition again, made a decision to move in with my last partner and her family. She is the one that I had painted and covered with the figure eights. I was still searching for that sense of family that I had never experienced. I was still hoping for someone to care enough to tuck me in at night. Unfortunately, I wasn't following the Instruction Book, God's Word –The Bible. I was still trying to manage the situation, instead of doing things God's way. The heart was somewhat willing, but my soul and body was weak.

I stopped the 1,200 pills per month and started eating organic food and then began taking natural supplements. I thought I had my life together, since I was no longer battling the demons of manic/bipolar episodes, heart disease, hypertension or any other physical illness. So, I moved in with Delilah, and we were going to start a business together. But, **God had another plan!**

I haven't been shy about sharing that I am given to visions. Shortly after I moved into this relationship, at a very intimate moment, I saw not the face of the woman I was with, but instead, an ancient demonic spirit. The face was melting, and it was like something from a horror movie! I could not believe my eyes.

Looking away did not make the vision go away. I had to get away, as I believed this to be clear direction from God!

Almost immediately, I started attending church and immersing myself in in God's word. Staying on the current pathway seemed to not be an option. Everything that could go wrong went wrong! My car started having mechanical problems – my computer would not work correctly my printer – stopped working and I had to buy a new one! My business was phone based, and there was no peace and quiet, in fact, I didn't even have a work space. This was the home of many, and there was much going on. Often teenagers were visiting – always playing their loud music and the mother of a woman living in the apartment below us was yelling at her husband from dawn to dark.

It took me only a few weeks to start packing. I believe God put it on my heart to move back to New Hampshire, so I packed up only my personal belongings and left **everything** else behind.

As I was leaving with the last armful of belongings, I shut the door behind me and brushed my feet at the door. I had no clue why I did that.

Looking back now, with the benefit of reading Scripture, I now know why. Jesus told his disciples, *"And if any place will not welcome you or will not listen to you, leave that place and shake the dust off your feet as a testimony against them." (Mark 6:11.)* I **knew** I did not belong there!

I really believe that God was enabling the changes in my life. I chose to listen to Him and change my lifestyle. God even allowed me to be completely emotionally detached as I left this relationship. I wanted to do the right things, and I was learning from God what the "right things" were. Learning is not always easy, and I had much more to learn from God in my new relationship with Him.

Food For Thought

There is a word – "repentance." It is one of those church words that seems like it belongs to a vocabulary set that only church people understand. Really it's a very simple concept. You cannot serve two masters at the same time. If God calls you to follow Him, you have to stop what you are doing, turn around from the direction you are going in order to follow Him. In essence, repentance is doing "an about face" and going in a totally opposite direction from the one you have been travelling.

Out of Bondage and Healed From Illnesses

I was bound by sin – tied up in a life that was a mess. God's Spirit did not have to, but thankfully kept pursuing me, tugging at my heart to turn from the bondage of sin and yield to His loving leadership.

God healed me from numerous illnesses that had plagued me for years. I have been freed of cancer, diabetes, Raynaud's disease, hypertension, high cholesterol, neuropathy, asthma, arthritis, stomach issues, severe nerve root damage, fibromyalgia, degenerative disc disease, extreme pain, and heart disease after my heart attack. I was in a wheel chair, and doctors told me I would not walk again, but I have walked just fine for years. My orthopedic doctor wanted to give me a hip replacement. God chose to heal that hip, as well.

God has set me free from the misdiagnosis of "bipolar" illness with its manic episodes. The theory of the medical profession is that people with "bipolar" illness suffer from a combination of an imbalance of chemicals in the brain, as well as abuse and/or stress, neglect and brokenness.

I believe that in my case it was misdiagnosed as a chemical imbalance when it was actually caused by my past neglect and abuse. Satan, who seeks to destroy us, was using this as his tool.

Every month, I was taking 1,200 pills. I agree that abuse,

neglect, and stress triggered my multiple illnesses and made them worse. However, what helped me more than anything (including pills!) was not counseling by medical professionals, but time spent in prayer and in Bible study.

I had tried in my own strength to overcome bipolar illness by using the regime recommended by my doctors. Both had failed me! I hated what I had become over the course of my lifetime. Remember: I was weak, timid, and sick with racing thoughts, could not sleep, and uncomfortable in my own skin. It was time to hand over the controls of my life to God.

When I took responsibility for my actions towards others and gave my anger over to Christ, He gave me a much more peaceful spirit. God didn't download everything immediately…but, He gently led me to understand that the way I had been living was not the "right way"… not His way! Eventually, He changed my desires taking away the dependencies that I had, and He even took away the loneliness.

I had been reading God's Word, the Bible, but I began to step up my study. I wanted to learn more about Him. He showed me in His Word that my body is His temple which is made to serve Him (1 Corinthians 3:16, 6:19), and that the only way to restore my body to good health was through a combination of His Divine healing and proper nutrition. I came to understand that poor eating habits had played a key role in destroying my body.

Once I gave everything to Christ, I became a new person, one that had new strength to overcome my old problems.

The Bible says, "*If anyone is in Christ, the new creation has come: The old has gone, the new is here!*" 2 Corinthians 5:17.

Christ gave me power to overcome abusive behaviors others had inflicted upon me. He showed me that I didn't have to follow my parents' bad examples, and could stop behaving like them. Likewise, God delivered me from my self-inflicted abuse and my bondage to the sins of addiction to drugs, alcohol, sex, and gambling. His power alone gave me the desire and ability to change after 40 years of homosexuality!

Food For Thought

God knit us together in our mother's womb making our bodies to work like fine pieces of equipment. The World pulls us, and because we are sinners, we veer from His ways. In doing so, we make a big mess of things, and it's not until we give Him our lives and let Him be in control, that we can follow His path of blessing for us. That's not to say, that the instant we give Him control, everything becomes perfect. Quite the contrary, life is a process. We continue to learn from God and grow until we die. Then we live eternally in perfection with Jesus, the Savior who rescued us!

God Pursued Me Until I
Finally Surrendered

People have told me I should have been walking with God a long time ago. I wish I knew then what I know now, but hindsight is 20/20. Salvation comes about through a combination of God initiating the relationship with us and our responding to His prompting. Jesus said in John 6:44 that, *"no one comes unto Him unless the Father draws them unto Him."*

You may feel unworthy of a relationship with God, but let me assure you of God's love for you! The Bible says, *"But God demonstrates his own love for us in this: While we were still sinners, Christ died for us."* Romans 5:8. There is nothing you have done that He hasn't seen before. There is no amount of sin or type of sin He didn't bear on the cross for you. The only sin He refuses to forgive is the sin of rejecting Him as your Savior and Lord.

He pursues us, and the fact is that he is willing to forgive us no matter how ugly our sin gets. There were many times that God tried to get my attention and I turned away. At the time, I could not see what He intended for my life. But, despite my rejections, God was faithful to pursue me and reach out to me until I finally responded and surrendered to His call.

Food For Thought

If becoming a Christian had been dependent upon something that I could do, I still would not be a Christian. Our worthiness is "as filthy rags". We cannot clean up our lives to be accepted by God. He is the one who cleans us up and gives us the power to change. And if a person is willing to make a change, God is willing to welcome him or her to Himself. It's really very simple, "He loved us and sent His Son to die for us." How much love is that?

A Warm Hug from the Holy Spirit

I believe I had a Divine visitation one snowy night during the winter of 2010. I was living on Ocean Boulevard in Hampton, New Hampshire, 107 steps from the ocean wall. I loved being there because the Lord provided beautiful sunrises and sunsets, many of which I photographed. Obviously, no camera does justice to the Lord's paintbrush. My memories are vivid of His awesome power moving within the ocean. I played over and over in my mind the tides coming in and going out, imagining it was Christ breathing.

I had been working with a friend from Las Vegas for three days on a study about angels. I was sitting at my desk pulling up information on my computer and was almost done with the study. All of a sudden, I had warmth on my right side and it felt so comfortable. A calm that was exciting came over me. I know that a person can have a fever, but fever is not confined to a certain spot. Fever covers the entire body, but this was only on my right side. I have no doubt that this was clearly God's Holy Spirit revealing Himself to me through His very warm presence. When the warm feeling came over me I did not immediately comprehend what was happening, nor did I anticipate the huge change that was about to take place in my life.

To my right, there was an incredibly fresh smell. The aroma was something almost indescribable to this day. God gave me a vivid memory of the scent. In my mind there were unforgettable images. I was experiencing wonderful aromas hard to describe. It was as though a panorama of beautiful scenes came flowing in procession through my mind:

- I beheld dew drops on thousands of long stem roses on an early sunny day, and breathed in the fresh scent.
- I beheld a waterfall as I was standing in front of it, waste-deep in clear blue water, watching in awe as the rainbows formed, surrounded by a beautiful glistening stone quarry. The freshness of the misty air was incredible.
- I beheld a rain forest with enormous green trees reaching toward the sky, as though the sun was coming back out after a quick thunderstorm, with birds on branches casting their shadows and singing songs of joy. As I beheld the rain forest, I smelled the bark and greenery, and as I watched the steam and heat come off the trees, it was an earthy smell, much like the fresh stirred soil of the forest.
- I beheld the shore line of the ocean after a thunderstorm, when the sand has been washed clean. The clouds had disappeared, and the waves had given off their warm mist, so much that I could feel it on my face.
- I beheld a mountain after a brief snow squall, when despite the inches of snow, the sun shines and the warmth penetrates the very breath you breathe. I smelled the fresh snow and the pines trees giving off their scent. It was like being in the middle of hundreds of Christmas trees after a rain.

Food For Thought

In Scripture, particularly the Old Testament, God revealed things to people with visions and dreams. When Jesus returned to Heaven, God gave the Holy Spirit to us as a comforter. Sometimes dream and visions have deep meanings that are intentionally being conveyed to us. <u>*Understanding of those visions and dreams comes from seeking comprehension in God's Word and through prayer.*</u>

Part 11

Accepting The New Me

Obedient Baptism

From the first moment that I heard the whisper in my ear, "lifestyle change," I was determined for my life to be different. You have to understand, I had tried to make a difference in my life in my own strength, and I couldn't do it and found it was going to take more than my will to bring forth the change needed.

Titus 3:3-5 beautifully describes how God generously poured out His love and mercy upon me. It says, *"At one time we too were foolish, disobedient, deceived and enslaved by all kinds of passions and pleasures…But when the kindness and love of God our Savior appeared, he saved us, not because of righteous things we had done, but because of his mercy."*

Jesus said, *"Come to me, all who are weary and burdened, and I will give you rest…and you will find rest for your souls. For my yoke is easy and my burden is light."* Matthew 11:28-30. The enormity and nature of my sin did not matter, because Jesus paid for it all at Calvary. *"…Christ died for the ungodly."* Romans 5:6. *"Christ Jesus came into the world to save sinners."* 1 Timothy 1:15. God sent Jesus *"to set the oppressed free."* Luke 4:18.

I accepted Jesus not only as my Savior but also as Lord (the One in charge of) my life. I gladly gave my life to Him for what He had done on the cross for me at Calvary by dying for my sins. I happily exchanged my old life for a new one, walking with Him, and have never regretted it for one second. So many people are willing to accept Christ as their Savior on their own terms, with reservations, but He made it clear that we must give our lives to Him without reservation. He said, "*Whoever finds their life will lose it, and whoever loses their life for my sake will find it.*" Matthew 10:39.

Being saved comes simply by believing and confessing Jesus as your Lord. The Bible says, "*…if you declare with your mouth, 'Jesus is Lord,' and believe in your heart that God raised him from the dead, you will be saved.*" Romans 10:9.

How amazing is He and how powerful is He, because He saved me from Hell and made me His child!

In the Gospels, (Matthew 3, Mark 1, Luke 3, and John 1), the scriptures tell us of Christ's baptism. I had been reading and studying the Bible and listening to teaching and preaching, and I wanted to be baptized, like Jesus had been.

The night before I was to be baptized, I got sick and ended up in the bed. I wasn't just sick, I was aching so badly that I practically had to crawl to the bathroom to take a hot shower and see if I could shake it off. I had a conversation with the Lord. Praying I asked, 'Lord, why is this happening?' Now I realize Satan, the enemy, was interfering with my obedience to Christ, trying to keep me from being baptized as planned.

Following a night of struggle, the next morning I opened my Bible and was encouraged by reading John 3:5-8, "*Jesus answered, "Very truly I tell you, no one can enter the kingdom of God unless they are born of water and the Spirit. Flesh gives birth to flesh, but the Spirit gives birth to spirit. You should not be surprised at my saying, 'You must be born again.' The wind blows wherever it pleases. You hear its sound, but you cannot tell where it comes from or where it is going. So it is with everyone born of the Spirit.*"

That day I was grateful to be baptized. I saw this as a symbolic act that showed Christ my obedience in following Him. My sins had already been forgiven and cleansed because of the blood of Jesus which He shed on the Cross. He washed me white as snow when I accepted Him as my Savior! Isn't it amazing, that red blood could wash black sins and make a person, white as snow! The Bible says that when we are saved our sins are removed from us *"as far as the east is from the west."* Psalm 103:12.

2 Corinthians 5:17 "Therefore, if anyone is in Christ, the new creation has come: The old has gone, the new is here!"

Food For Thought

In Baptism, we identify with Christ, our Lord, who died physically, was buried, and was resurrected. Being immersed, we are demonstrating we have died to our old selves. Coming up out of the water represents we have experienced newness of life only Christ can give. Baptism symbolizes death and burial of the old sinful life and resurrection of the new life Christ gives the one who believes in Him.

The Sand Dollar

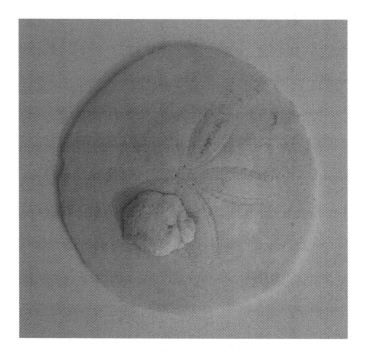

Immediately following my baptism, I went walking on the beach. It had become a habit to walk a twelve mile stretch on the beach, taking time to process what I had heard and appreciate God's beauty. There was such a drawing of the Spirit to walk with Him there, and the closeness I experienced was so precious to me.

This particular day, as I was walking, the wave came in like a sheet of glass. Looking down, there was a single sand dollar. There was no other debris, no other shells, no stones – there was only the single sand dollar. If I had not been looking down, I would have walked right past it or possibly even stepped on it. What was there caught my eye as there seemed to be something stuck on this little thing of beauty. I tried to pick it off, and that's when I saw the image.

I had been asking God to show more of Himself to me, and He did in a very real and tangible way! I found myself in tears. I felt like He had sent a personal message to me.

The sand dollar had a perfect image of a lamb's head on it. Actually, depending on one's perception, there are a number of images: the lamb's head, which was facing toward the right, a ram's head, facing toward the left, and the number 7 in the area of the lamb's eye. What a beautiful message, reiterating that Jesus is the Lamb of God. I believe that this was the Lord's confirmation of His presence, my salvation, and His miraculous power. This experience served as His affirmation of my obedience in baptism.

Food For Thought

You've probably heard someone, at some point in your lifetime, say, "God works in mysterious ways, His wonders to perform." Sometimes He uses the smallest, most common things to speak to our hearts. On this day, I had followed Christ's example – I had been baptized; confirming that I was one of His sheep, if you will. It had been four years since I had accepted Christ as my Savior. In Scripture, He tells us that He is willing to leave the fold, and go searching for even one little lost lamb. I was so lost – and He sought me out and brought me to safety. "He is my Shepherd; I shall not want."

Part 12

Following His Lead

On Fire

From that point on, I was truly changed and no longer the person that I used to be. My shyness and timid tendencies were a thing of the past. I had an inexplicable desire to learn, to grow, to be able to help others find what I had found. I wanted everyone to understand that they did not have to live in captivity and suffering!

I was not just dunked in the water. I was baptized into the fellowship of a church – a living breathing body of believers. One of the deacon's wives began to mentor me – to lead and guide me in a better understanding of what a "life pleasing to the Lord" really meant. I was not a stranger to reading the Bible, but I began to study in a way that helped me to deepen my relationship with Christ. What I had only "read about" began to make sense, to come alive within me. I was on fire for the Lord and I wanted everyone that I came in contact with to feel the warmth and freedom that I was feeling.

I became involved with the goings-on of the church, with food preparation for classes, with landscaping, helping around the homes of various members, and outings for fun and recreation. I looked for ways I could be involved and spend time with my brothers and sisters in the family of Christ, my new family. This was not a dysfunctional family. This was a family that would not let you down or abuse you. I don't want to paint an unreal picture – there probably is not a perfect church. People are made of flesh and bone and have the propensity to let other people down – but, I did not experience that in this church. These people that were my first experience in the family of God were loving and nurturing toward me. I had never experienced the calm and joy of being around others that I found in this place. I was sure that I had found a home.

I was so surprised when I began feeling a pull in another direction. I was asking God for His direction in my life, and He began opening new doors for me – it was up to me to walk through them or remain where I was.

Food For Thought

John Wesley, a knowledgeable and often quoted forefather of religion, once remarked, "When you set yourself on fire, people love to come see you burn." That is a wild saying, but so true. People love to get close to dramatic situations. I understand what Reverend Wesley was saying, but I had not set myself on fire. I was ignited by the Holy Spirit and fueled by the power of God as I followed Jesus as His disciple. Anything that was showing through was not drama – it was genuine – it was a spiritual zeal.

Sharing the Experience

I began studying ***Experiencing God – Knowing and Doing the Will of God*** by Henry Blackaby. This book made a profound impact on my life, and I highly recommend it. It teaches that many of us make the mistake of choosing our own projects and tasks to do rather than seeking how we can join in God's activities. An important Biblical principle to follow is finding where the Lord is already working and joining Him in what He is doing. I began to follow this principle. I asked Him to put people in my life each and every day that needed Him. Then, I didn't sit at home and wait for them to come to me; I got out and made myself available. I didn't try to make it happen, but I did keep my eyes open for opportunities and I went well equipped.

The outcome is outstanding. My timidity has become a thing of the past. I am now bold enough to grasp opportunities to walk up to a person and ask, "Are you a believer?" They often ask, "A believer in what?" which gives me an opportunity to share the wonderful story of God's plan of salvation.

I often see God working in the lives of hurting people and very often they can relate to my past. I first talk about repentance, and people are shocked to see that they have violated Gods laws as set forth in the Ten Commandments. Most people have heard of the commandments, but don't relate to them in simple everyday terms such as putting money and possessions ahead of God, taking the Lord's name in vain, dishonoring one's parents, or lying, stealing, adultery, envy, or lusting after something that is not yours, to be against God's word.

I go on to ask, "Where do you think you would go if Judgment Day came today?" Most everyone realizes that there does come a point in time when they will face death when they take just a moment to think about it. After that, I have a moment to share the provision that God made for them to spend Eternity in Heaven, through the gift of His only begotten Son, Jesus, on the cross.

I have felt a strong calling to be involved in women's prison ministry. You find many people in prisons with dysfunctional backgrounds like mine.

God made it clear to me that many are in prison for making poor choices, and Satan has a strong hold on them because he wants possession of their souls. You see, God offers the free gift of salvation through giving His Son to die for our sins. Notice I didn't say 'your' sins…I include myself, too.

The Bible says in Romans, that "all have sinned and come short of the glory of God." God will not force Himself on anyone – that was a strange concept to me – not to have things forced on me. God is a gentleman, He makes the provision, but it's up to the individual to accept or reject Him. And, if we choose to reject God's gift, Satan *takes* possession, period. He is certainly **not** a gentleman!

Food For Thought

I can't tell you how many times I've had someone tell me, when I begin asking them about their salvation, that they say they pray to God. In fact, they pray and pray and He never answers. They act as though they are disappointed in Him. If you are seeking Him, He will reach out to you. However, the first specific prayer that God is willing to hear and answer is the prayer that acknowledges sin in your life and your need of a Savior! When you have a personal relationship with God in Christ, He longs to hear your prayer and answer, because you are now His child.

If we have cherished sins in our lives, and refused to give them up, or if we are doing things we should not be doing, and are knowingly disobeying Him, we cannot expect Him to answer our prayers. He cannot answer our prayers if we have sins in our lives that are unconfessed, or if we are hanging on to cherished sins. Also, if we refuse to forgive others who have wronged us, God cannot hear us. (See Matthew 6:12 and Ephesians 4:32.)

Move to North Carolina

After having lived in New Hampshire for 50 years, I recently moved to a small community in the mountains of western North Carolina. When the opportunity to move to North Carolina came, I prayed for three months, and when God paved the way, I moved in faith that God was going to use me. I had asked the Lord to please give me a place I could call home because all I wanted to do with my life was to glorify God.

God had convicted me to be transparent with everyone that I encountered in my new walk. I was gay for 40 years, and I did not change me...**God changed me!** He broke my chains and saved my soul. I wasn't fully aware at the time that God had led me to a place where I would have opportunities to share my faith with others in the gay lifestyle. I have made friends and shared my faith by telling my story. God has blessed me with many spiritual children that I love and nurture in the Lord!

Where I live feels like home to me. I have a new church family and many new brothers and sisters in Christ who encourage me in so many ways. My pastor has supported me in sharing my testimony, not only in my own community, but in other areas as well.

I had asked the Lord to please give me a place I could call home because all I wanted to do with my life was to glorify God.

Food For Thought

God is interested in the smallest details of our lives...everything from where we live to what we eat. At the table, we ask Him to bless our food, but He does want us to pay attention to any food or substance which would harm the bodies He has given us. Eat smart. Be smart.

Part 13

Living As A
Changed Woman

Forgiveness

Imagine how difficult it has been for me to forgive my father and mother, as well as all the men who abused both my baby sister and me. Can you imagine how hard it was to forgive myself, as well, for the things I have done?

Forgiveness is not something that God made optional for us. Jesus made it absolutely clear that if we can't forgive, God won't forgive us. If God can forgive us, we can forgive others. It is that simple. Do you have someone you need to forgive, including yourself? As I did, you can give it to the only person that can handle it all, Christ.

I found peace with my past when I was finally able to rid myself of the hate and anger against those I held responsible for all the devastation in my life. The hate and anger was eating away at me, and I didn't need it to occupy my time and energy anymore. It was keeping me in bondage.

At a friend's recommendation, I made a list of everyone I held responsible for my past that was affecting my future in a negative way. My name was at the top of the list. It wasn't necessary to write down what each had done to me, because I had re-lived the events countless times in my mind. After writing all the names down and looking the list over, I simply crumpled the piece of paper in my hand and pictured myself handing that crumpled piece of paper over to Jesus. I envisioned Jesus standing in front of me. He was glowing and I was in tears, saying, "Lord, I can't do this anymore, and I need your forgiveness and help to forgive!" It's as though I heard Him say, "Your sins are forgiven. Just leave the others to me!" By God's grace and with His help, I forgave them once and for all. Satan tries to take away my joy by taking me back to that unforgiving state. The memories occasionally do resurface, but I have forgiven the people involved, and God renews my joy when that happens.

My mom had deep regrets for not protecting me and my baby sis any better than she did, and I believe she tried to make amends with the Lord before she died. Her repentance made it much easier to forgive her.

Food For Thought

Perhaps you need to forgive yourself for something that has you in bondage. Maybe there are people in your life that you need to forgive. (Matthew 6:15) "But if you do not forgive others their sins, your Father will not forgive your sins."

God stands ready to forgive you and help you forgive others. Have a heart-to-heart with Him as I did. It will change your life and bring you joy.

My Sexuality Today

Recovering from my past is not easy, as you can imagine. Even though God has delivered me from the bondage of homosexuality, it is impossible to erase my mind from the memories of past relationships. I am now recognizing the source of temptation when it comes my way. Satan likes to use our memories and lustful nature as a primary source of temptation. He works that way because he doesn't want us to have a blessed relationship with God through Jesus. **He wants to destroy our lives**.

Remember, Jesus said, "The thief (Satan) cometh not, but for to steal, and to kill, and to destroy: I am come that they might have **life**, and that they might have it more **abundant**ly." (John 10:10) Satan would destroy us, but **Jesus wants to give us life!** Can you see the difference?

Temptation is not a sin, as Jesus Himself was tempted for 40 days and 40 nights in the wilderness and remained sinless! We all daily face temptations and I am no exception. God promises every believer victory over temptation. I praise God for giving me spiritual strength for every spiritual battle through prayer and immersing myself in God's word, the Bible.

You are not responsible for the feelings you have (temptation is not a sin) as long as they neither turn into lustful thoughts nor sexual behavior. Temptation is nothing but a suggestion to sin, a prompting to do something wrong. The progression of temptation into sin is described in James 1:14-15, which says, "...but each person is tempted when they are dragged away by their own evil desire and enticed. Then, after desire has conceived, it gives birth to sin; and sin, when it is full-grown, gives birth to death."

We have the power within us to not give way to sin, because of His enabling grace He has given us in His Son! The Lord promises us supernatural help in our hour of temptation. "And God is faithful; he will not let you be tempted beyond what you can bear. But when you are tempted, he will also provide a way out so that you can endure it." 1 Corinthians 10:13.

We actually sin when we yield in our heart to the temptation, that is, choose to sin. Sin can take the form of an action, but we can sin even in our thinking. For example, Jesus said, "But I say unto you, that whosoever looketh on a woman to lust after her hath committed adultery with her already in his heart. (Matthew 5:28)

Food for Thought

When you are faced with temptation, recognize its source and trust this promise of God: (James 4:7) "Submit yourselves therefore to God. Resist the devil, and he will flee from you." The word 'resisting' means willfully turning away from that temptation. God will bless you as He strengthens you, making it easier the next time.

Part 14

Cleared From Confusion

I Was Confused

I thought I was born gay. If I, at the age of ten, felt drawn to the same sex, I figured God had made me that way and there was no changing it. Many people struggle with questions about this. Not knowing what God had to say about it in His Word, I had continued in the homosexual lifestyle for 40 years.

Leviticus 18 contains God's judgment on sexual sins, and the first chapter of Romans describes God's wrath against mankind for rejecting Him, even though He has done everything to reveal Himself. After rejecting God, people turned from God to all sorts of sins, including sexual immorality.

Romans 1:24-32 "24 Therefore God gave them over in the sinful desires of their hearts to sexual impurity for the degrading of their bodies with one another. 25 They exchanged the truth about God for a lie, and worshiped and served created things rather than the Creator – who is forever praised. Amen. 26"Because of this, God gave them over to shameful lusts. Even their women exchanged natural sexual relations for unnatural ones. 27 In the same way the men also abandoned natural relations with women and were inflamed with lust for one another. Men committed shameful acts with other men, and received in themselves the due penalty for their error.

28 Furthermore, just as they did not think it worthwhile to retain the knowledge of God, so God gave them over to a depraved mind, so that they do what ought not to be done.

²⁹ They have become filled with every kind of wickedness, evil, greed, and depravity. They are full of envy, murder, strife, deceit, and malice. They are gossips, ³⁰ slanderers, God-haters, insolent, arrogant and boastful; they invent ways of doing evil; they disobey their parents; ³¹ they have no understanding, no fidelity, no love, no mercy. ³² Although they know God's righteous decree that those who do such things deserve death, they not only continue to do these very things but also approve of those who practice them."

God will forgive any sin, except for your rejection of His Only Son, Christ Jesus, whom He sent to die on the cross to save us from sin. Jesus is the only avenue to a relationship with God and to Heaven. He said, "I am the way, the truth, and the life." God will only recognize you as His child through your faith in Christ for salvation.

(John 3:16-18) "¹⁶ For God so loved the world that he gave his one and only Son, that whoever believes in him shall not perish but have eternal life. ¹⁷ For God did not send his Son into the world to condemn the world, but to save the world through him. ¹⁸ Whoever believes in him is not condemned, but whoever does not believe stands condemned already because they have not believed in the name of God's one and only Son."

Do you recognize the truth in this scripture?

The Bible gives the steps to receiving God's forgiveness for sins. Here it is in a nutshell…

Here is how you can receive Christ:

1. Admit your need (I am a sinner).
2. Be willing to turn from your sins (repent).

3. Believe that Jesus Christ died for you on the Cross and rose from the grave.

4. Through prayer, invite Jesus Christ to come in and control your life. (Receive Him as Lord and Savior.)

We are all sinners.

Romans 3:23 says "For all have sinned and fallen short of the glory of God."

God says we are all sinners, and – even if we think of ourselves as "good," we will not go to heaven without receiving Christ. Only forgiven sinners will enter heaven.

Sin results in spiritual death and hell.

Romans 6:23 says, "For the wages of sin is death." --So God, because of His love for us, sent Jesus to die on the cross to pay the penalty of our sins. Romans 5:8 says, "But God commanded His love towards us, in while we were yet sinners, Christ died for us." Jesus took our punishment for sin.

To receive Jesus: To receive Jesus's sacrifice for our sins we must not only believe that He is God's Son, but ask Him to save us from our sins and rule and reign in and over our lives, thus becoming our Savior and Lord.

Romans 10:9-10 says: "That if you confess with your mouth the Lord Jesus Christ and believe in your heart that God has raised Him from the dead, you shall be saved."

God's gift to us is His saving us if we ask Him. Romans 6:23 says, "For the wages of sin is death, but the gift of God is eternal life in Christ Jesus our Lord."

When should I be saved? NOW! Right now! You never know when you might die or be killed. And after that, it's too late to be saved, and you will go to hell forever and ever. Hebrews 3:7 says "Today, if you will hear His voice, do not harden your hearts." Also, 2 Corinthians 6:3 says, "Behold, NOW is the accepted time; behold, now is the day of salvation."

Is there anyone else or any other way to be saved? NO. Since God created us, it stands to reason that only God can save us from our sins. And God has chosen Jesus as the way to do this. Acts 4:12 says, "Nor is there salvation found in any other, for there is no other name under heaven given among men by which we must be saved."

He is knocking at your door. Jesus said "Behold I stand at the door (your heart) and knock. If anyone hears My voice and opens the door, I will come in to him and dine with him, and he with Me." Revelation 3:20. In other words, Jesus WILL save you if you let Him into your heart and life.

Will you ask Jesus into your heart today? Just pray this prayer (and truly mean it), and you will be saved: Dear God: I realize that I'm a sinner and I can't save myself. I believe you sent your Son Jesus to die on the cross to take the penalty of my sins. I ask Jesus now to come into my life and save my soul, to be my Savior and my Friend. I need you in my life, because my life is meaningless without You. I accept the free gift of salvation You offer me. Please lead, guide, protect, and direct my life from this point forward. Thank You for forgiving my sins and giving me a new life and a fresh start. In Jesus name I pray, Amen.

My experience:

I, like you, had to accept what God's word says about my sin and recognize where I was headed for eternity without God in my life. I examined the above scriptures, studied and meditated on them. God spoke to my heart through them, and I recognized the truth of God's word. After praying a similar prayer as stated above, I became a new person. (2 Corinthians 5:17) My old life has been exchanged for my new life in Christ, to the glory of His name and the work He has done on my behalf. My prayer for you is that you will have this same experience and allow Christ to give you new life, as well as His joy, His comfort, and peace in your life.

Food For Thought

I was confused. You may be, too. You don't have to be confused anymore. Remember this:

*(*1 Corinthians 14:33*) "For God is not the author of confusion, but of peace, as in all churches of the saints." God gives us the way out of our confusion. Once we pray to receive Christ as Savior and Lord of our lives, we become "saints" and experience God's peace. Our past confusion will become a mere memory!*

After Receiving Christ, What Next?

God's assurance to you is found in His Word.

If you prayed to ask Jesus into your heart, **the Bible says...**

"Everyone who calls on the name of the Lord will be saved." Romans 10:13

"For it is by grace you have been saved, through faith--and this not from yourselves, it is the gift of God--not by works, so that no one can boast." Ephesians 2:8-9

"He who has the Son has life; he who does not have the Son of God does not have life. I write these things to you who believe in the name of the Son of God so that you may know that you have eternal life." 1 John 5:12-13

Receiving Christ, we are born into God's family through the supernatural work of the Holy Spirit who indwells every believer. This is called regeneration, or the "new birth."

You are a new person now!
"Therefore, <u>if anyone is in Christ</u>, the new creation has come: The old has gone, the new is here!" 2 Corinthians 5:17

This is just the beginning of a wonderful new life in Christ. To deepen your relationship with Him:

1. Read your Bible every day to know Christ better.
2. Talk to God in prayer every day. His promised never to leave you. Envision Him at your side as you pray.
3. Tell others about Christ.
4. Worship, fellowship, and serve with other Christians in a church where Christ is preached.
5. As Christ's representative in a needy world, demonstrate your new life by your love and concern for others.

If you've just made this commitment to Christ, further spiritual help and information about being a Christian is available at these two trustworthy websites:

1. http://www.billygraham.org
2. **http://www.mostimportantthing.org**

So now that you have committed your life to Christ, He commands each new believer to be baptized, symbolic of your death to your old life, burial, and resurrection....His cleansing of your sin and giving you a brand new life. I have found that new believers are eager to follow the Lord's admonition to be baptized.

Baptism is an act of obedience to one of Jesus' final instructions before leaving earth. He said, "Therefore go and make disciples (disciplined followers) of all nations, baptizing them in the name of the Father and of the Son and of the Holy Spirit..." Matthew 28:19.

God's self-sacrificing love is the main characteristic of His children and He does not expect us to live out our faith alone, but in a loving community of believers. God told us, "Love one another as I have loved you." John 13:34

As a new child of God, you will still sin sometimes, and Jesus will forgive you. All that you need to do is confess your sin to God, and He will forgive you and purify you from all unrighteousness. (See 1 John 1:9 which was written to Christians.) However, as we grow in Christ, the difference is we sin less and less. Why? Because Christ is working in us as we trust Him to make us more like Him all the time. Scripture teaches that the true believer will not stay in sin.

Please understand. There is no need to be re-baptized or celebrate communion each time you sin. Don't be tricked into believing that a ceremony saves you. **Salvation is a matter of what happens in the heart.**

Part 15

Closing Thoughts

Turning Over a New Leaf

Did you wonder about the book title? The term "to turn over a new leaf" is used to refer to making a new start. From the sound of it, one might think that this phrase is related to freshly budding green leaves in the spring, which carry a pleasant image of renewal and fresh starts. The term actually refers to turning the page of a book, however, and it dates to the 1500s.

In the 1500s in England, students used to write in pen and ink. It got pretty messy, and if they tried to correct work, it had to be done by scratching out the wrong word and writing the correct word above it. If you did that a number of times, you had a very, very messy page. A single page in a book was called a "leaf", – hence, turning over a new leaf meant turning to a new, blank page. It gradually came to mean "starting over again" which eventually included many areas other than school work. The implication is that one is turning over the previous page from bad behavior, and starting anew on a fresh page.

After prayer, my pastor and wife suggested my book title, primarily based on what they had seen in my life. This title relates to Biblical teaching about new life in Christ. By now, you should know that 2 Corinthians 5:17 is one of my favorite scriptures. My old life you read about is dead and gone. Did you see the dead leaves on the cover? That was me....one horrific mess! Now my life is fresh and new like a green leaf compared to those dead leaves.

Here are two Bible passages that clearly teach that Christ lives in the believer, giving His power to the believer to live His way. I know that He chose me to be His servant and that He is expecting me to be obedient. I also know I do not have the strength within myself to do this on my own! As Jesus said, "I am the vine; you are the branches. If a man remains in me and I in Him, he will bear much fruit; apart from me you can do nothing." (John 15:5)

The second passage that teaches that God supplies the strength to live a good and productive life that is pleasing to Him is found in the 1st Psalm. There is a contrast between those who delight in the Lord and those who try to live their own way without Him. Read it and see the strong contrast!

Psalm 1

*[1] Blessed is the one who does not walk in step with the wicked or stand in the way that sinners take or sit in the company of mockers, [2] but whose delight is in the law of the LORD, and who meditates on his law day and night. [3] That person is like a tree planted by streams of water, which yields its fruit in season and **whose leaf does not wither** – whatever they do prospers. [4] Not so the wicked! They are like chaff that the wind blows away. [5] Therefore the wicked will not stand in the judgment, nor sinners in the assembly of the righteous. [6] For the LORD watches over the way of the righteous, but the way of the wicked leads to destruction.*

A Forever Changed Life

Thank you for allowing me to share my story with you. I have discovered nothing fills the void in my life (not family, relationships, materialism, drugs, alcohol, and all the rest this world offers) like Jesus fills it! I will never turn back now! He is completing me and satisfies me. He can do the same for you. Let Him transform you and give you meaning and purpose for living! Then you will have a new life and your own wonderful story to tell, too!

Please share this book with others who are suffering at the hands of their own bad choices and seeking hope for positive change in their lives.

Feel free to connect with me through email at terileef@hotmail.com.

As the Lord leads, I am available for speaking engagements.

If you have interest in holistic nutritional supplements, please contact me at the above email address, as well.